INSIDE THE NBA

NEW ORLEANS PELICANS

BY TOM GLAVE

SportsZone

An Imprint of Abdo Publishing
abdobooks.com

abdobooks.com

Published by Abdo Publishing, a division of ABDO, PO Box 398166, Minneapolis, Minnesota 55439. Copyright © 2023 by Abdo Consulting Group, Inc. International copyrights reserved in all countries. No part of this book may be reproduced in any form without written permission from the publisher. SportsZone™ is a trademark and logo of Abdo Publishing.

Printed in the United States of America, North Mankato, Minnesota.
052022
092022

Cover Photo: Jonathan Bachman/Getty Images Sport/Getty Images
Interior Photos: Melinda Nagy/Shutterstock Images, 1; Chris Graythen/Getty Images Sport/Getty Images, 4, 18; Zach Bolinger/Icon Sportswire/SPTSW/AP Images, 7; Julio Cortez/AP Images, 8; Gerald Herbert/AP Images, 10, 13, 23, 32; Kirby Lee/LEEKI/AP Images, 14; Bill Haber/AP Images, 16; Layne Murdoch/National Basketball Association/Getty Images, 20; Mark J. Terrill/AP Images, 24; Dave Martin/AP Images, 27; Scott Threlkeld/AP Images, 29; G Fiume/Getty Images Sport/Getty Images, 34; David J. Phillip/AP Images, 37; Alex Brandon/AP Images, 38; Stephen Lew/Icon Sportswire/SPTSW/AP Images, 39; Ronald Martinez/Getty Images Sport/Getty Images, 41

Editor: Charlie Beattie
Series Designer: Joshua Olson

Library of Congress Control Number: 2021951648

Publisher's Cataloging-in-Publication Data

Names: Glave, Tom, author.
Title: New Orleans Pelicans / by Tom Glave
Description: Minneapolis, Minnesota : Abdo Publishing, 2023 | Series: Inside the NBA | Includes online resources and index.
Identifiers: ISBN 9781532198366 (lib. bdg.) | ISBN 9781098272012 (ebook)
Subjects: LCSH: New Orleans Pelicans (Basketball team)--Juvenile literature. | Basketball--Juvenile literature. | Professional sports--Juvenile literature. | Sports franchises--Juvenile literature.
Classification: DDC 796.32364--dc23

TABLE OF CONTENTS

CHAPTER ONE
WE WANT ZION 4

CHAPTER TWO
BAYOU BASKETBALL 14

CHAPTER THREE
BOURBON STREET BALLERS 24

CHAPTER FOUR
BIG MOMENTS IN THE BIG EASY 34

TIMELINE 42
TEAM FACTS 44
TEAM TRIVIA 45
GLOSSARY 46
MORE INFORMATION 47
ONLINE RESOURCES 47
INDEX 48
ABOUT THE AUTHOR 48

CHAPTER ONE

WE WANT ZION

New Orleans basketball fans were still playing the waiting game. For years they had hoped for a star who could turn their Pelicans into consistent winners. In the summer of 2019, they thought they had their man in rookie forward Zion Williamson. However, a knee injury delayed his National Basketball Association (NBA) debut until January 2020.

It was January 22 when Williamson finally suited up. The Pelicans were hosting the San Antonio Spurs. A sellout crowd at Smoothie King Center erupted when Williamson was introduced as a starter. The cheers soon became more muted. The rookie barely played in the first quarter. The same thing happened in the second quarter, and then the third. In the few minutes he was on the court, Williamson wasn't very effective. Through three quarters his stat line read: 12 minutes, five points, four turnovers. The Pelicans trailed the Spurs 94–82.

New Orleans Pelicans forward Zion Williamson, *right*, drives against the San Antonio Spurs on January 22, 2020.

It looked as if the New Orleans fans would have to wait at least one more night for Williamson to shine.

THE HYPE

Excitement around Williamson's basketball skill had been growing for years. No one had seen anything like him on the floor. At 6 feet, 6 inches and 284 pounds, he was built like a football defensive lineman. But he had the shooting touch and quickness of an NBA guard. He spent his high school days in South Carolina as an internet sensation because of his big dunks. Then he made nightly highlights during his single year of college at Duke University.

Williamson's college season nearly ended with a knee injury. His foot slipped out of his shoe early in a game against rival North Carolina on February 20, 2019. Williamson suffered a twisted knee. But he returned three weeks later to help Duke win the Atlantic Coast Conference (ACC) Tournament. Williamson averaged 27 points and 10 rebounds during that run. After the season was over, he declared for the NBA Draft. Williamson was sure to be the top pick. The only question was to which team.

TOP CHOICE

The Pelicans struggled to a 33–49 record in 2018–19. That mark was bad enough to keep them out of the playoffs for the

Williamson's size and explosiveness made him an exciting NBA prospect during his one season at Duke University.

Williamson, *right*, poses with NBA commissioner Adam Silver after being drafted first overall in 2019.

sixth time in eight years. But it was not bad enough to give New Orleans the best chance at winning the draft lottery. Six teams had worse records. Also, in 2019 the NBA changed the lottery system. The three worst teams had an even better chance of winning it than before. But it was the Pelicans' lucky day. One month later, at the draft, the team surprised no one by taking Williamson with that first pick.

He looked the part during the preseason. Williamson averaged 23.3 points and 6.5 rebounds in four games. He hit 71 percent of his shots. Then disaster struck when he had surgery on a torn meniscus on October 21. The injury kept Williamson out until January.

SLOW START, ELECTRIC FINISH

Williamson was finally ready to start against the Spurs. A crowd of 18,365 fans packed into the arena to see him. But through three quarters he had played only 11 minutes, 41 seconds. Head coach Alvin Gentry was easing him back into action. He did not want Williamson injuring his knee again.

New Orleans trailed San Antonio 99–91 as the clock hit 9:00 left in the game. Williamson still had not provided the fans the thrill they came for. Even worse, Gentry was calling for reserve Nicolò Melli to check in. At the next stop in play, Williamson was heading to the bench again.

Watching Zion

Pelicans fans were not the only ones excited for Zion Williamson's first game. Normally the team hands out 25 media passes for a Pelicans home game. On January 22, 2020, New Orleans had 165 media members at Smoothie King Center.

Williamson played only 18 minutes in his NBA debut but scored 22 points and added seven rebounds.

But then Pelicans guard Lonzo Ball kicked a pass to Williamson at the top of the key. Williamson stepped back and drilled an open three-pointer. The crowd rose to celebrate. The young star was not done. On the next possession he moved into the lane and spun away from defender DeMar DeRozan.

Ball lobbed a pass from outside the three-point line. Williamson snatched the alley-oop pass out of the air and laid it in. The crowd roared even louder.

When New Orleans got back on offense Williamson found himself wide open at the three-point line again. After he drilled another shot, the crowd exploded. Mark Jackson, broadcasting the game for ESPN, appealed for Williamson to stay in.

"If I'm Zion Williamson, I'm looking over at the bench and saying, 'Keep me in,'" Jackson said.

At that very moment, Melli got up and walked back to the bench. Gentry was going to see what Williamson could do.

The next time down the court, Williamson took a pass in the paint. He made a move to the basket, but his layup was blocked. Williamson was able to get the rebound, rise again, and hit a reverse layup. The Pelicans' fans were on their feet.

Williamson responded by knocking down three-point shots on each of New Orleans' next two possessions. He had scored 16 points in a row for his team. It had taken the young forward only 2 minutes and 34 seconds to do it.

San Antonio quickly took back the lead. Gentry wanted his team to call timeout. He wanted to sub out Williamson again. But Ball didn't listen. He brought the ball across half-court and ran a pick-and-roll with Williamson. The big forward was fouled after catching Ball's pass.

As Williamson stepped to the foul line, the packed Smoothie King Center shouted chants of "M-V-P!" at the young star. Williamson hit his second free throw. He had scored 17 consecutive points for New Orleans.

The next time up the floor, Ball did call timeout. Williamson walked off the floor to one last ovation from the crowd. He did not return for the rest of the game as the Spurs won 121–117.

Throughout the final five minutes of the loss, the home crowd chanted, "We want Zion!" But Gentry stuck to his plan and refused to put Williamson back in. After the game the coach was criticized for his decision.

Williamson was more focused on the crowd's reaction to his special night. His scoring spree tied him with forward Brandon Ingram as New Orleans' leading scorer in the game.

"It was everything I dreamed of except for the losing," Williamson said after the game. "Just the energy the crowd brought, the energy the city brought, it was electric, and I'm just grateful that they did that."

Williamson reacts after hitting a three-pointer during his fourth-quarter scoring streak against San Antonio.

CHAPTER TWO

BAYOU BASKETBALL

Professional basketball arrived in New Orleans in 2002, but it wasn't the first time. The New Orleans Jazz had played there from 1974 through 1979. But the team won very few games and drew very small crowds. They moved to Salt Lake City after the 1978–79 season and kept the Jazz nickname.

A decade later, a new team popped up in Charlotte, North Carolina. Local entrepreneur George Shinn wanted to get a team into the league. He and his business partners paid $32.5 million to the NBA and founded the Charlotte Hornets in 1987.

When the Hornets took the court during the 1988–89 season, they were immediately popular. North Carolina had long been a hotbed of college basketball. Top programs such as the University of North Carolina, North Carolina State University, Wake Forest University, and Duke University played

Forward P. J. Brown was one of many key players who made the move with the team from Charlotte to New Orleans.

Owner George Shinn moved the Hornets from his hometown of Charlotte to New Orleans.

just hours from Charlotte. Fans supported the new professional team in huge numbers. The Charlotte Coliseum was one of the NBA's newest stadiums. It was also the biggest. The arena held 24,000 fans. The popular Hornets sold it out for 364 consecutive games.

After some early struggles, the Hornets started winning in the early 1990s. They were led by two of the game's biggest young stars. Forward Larry Johnson and center Alonzo Mourning looked like a winning combination. But after a few years together, the two stars started squabbling. Both were eventually traded.

The Hornets stayed competitive, but they never made it out of the second playoff round. By the late 1990s, another squabble was brewing. Shinn's arena was state-of-the-art in the late 1980s. But by the end of the 1990s, it was outdated. The owner wasn't able to convince the city to help finance a new home for the Hornets. Fans, angry with Shinn, stopped showing up at games.

In 2001–02, the Hornets were last in NBA attendance. What had been one of the league's most popular teams was in trouble. Shinn thought his best move was to relocate the team. The Hornets left for New Orleans after the season.

NEW CITY, SAME RESULTS

The Hornets arrived in New Orleans as a playoff-ready team. They showed it on their first night in New Orleans Arena. The city's former team, the Jazz, was in town on October 30, 2002. Point guard Baron Davis's 21 points and 10 assists led a rout. New Orleans won the game 100–75.

Davis missed 32 games that season with injuries. But All-Star forward Jamal Mashburn carried the Hornets to the playoffs. New Orleans won its last five games of the year to clinch a postseason berth. The Hornets were bounced in the first round by the Philadelphia 76ers. After the series, head coach Paul Silas was fired.

Tim Floyd replaced Silas, but the Hornets did not improve. Davis once again missed time with injuries in 2003–04. This time, Mashburn joined him on the sidelines. The forward played only 19 games. At 41–41, the Hornets snuck into

The Hornets had a star point guard in Baron Davis when they moved to New Orleans, but injuries often kept him off the floor during his three seasons in the team's new home.

the playoffs. Playing without Mashburn, the Hornets lost to the Miami Heat in the first round. Just as in the season before, the head coach was fired. Out went Floyd, and in came former NBA guard Byron Scott.

The next season saw New Orleans on the move again—but not out of the city. The NBA introduced a new team, the Charlotte Bobcats, in the summer of 2004. The Hornets had been playing in the NBA's Eastern Conference. When the Bobcats arrived, New Orleans moved to the West.

The season was a total disaster. The Hornets started 2–29. Mashburn and Davis were both traded in February. New Orleans sank to 18–64 by the end of the season and needed to start over with a remade roster.

A TEAM WITHOUT A CITY

The low finish left the Hornets in a good spot in the draft lottery. They earned the fourth pick overall and chose point guard Chris Paul from Wake Forest. However, fans in New Orleans had to wait years to see him play.

On August 29, 2005, Hurricane Katrina devastated the Gulf Coast of the United States. New Orleans suffered intense damage due to flooding and high winds. New Orleans Arena was damaged as well. With the city destroyed, its sports teams had no place to play.

Shinn and the NBA quickly made arrangements for the Hornets. They moved their headquarters to Oklahoma City for the upcoming 2005–06 season.

The Hornets were embraced by fans in Oklahoma City and greeted with sell-out crowds. But the schedule still included

The Hornets played their first regular-season game in Oklahoma City on November 1, 2005, against the Sacramento Kings. New Orleans won 93–67.

four games in Louisiana. The Hornets played once at Louisiana State University (LSU) in Baton Rouge and three times at New Orleans Arena. They went 1–3 in those games and finished the season 38–44. But there were some bright spots on the court, notably from Paul. He was named Rookie of the Year.

The plan was to return to New Orleans as soon as the city could take the team back. That took longer than expected. The league announced in January 2006 that the Hornets would spend another season in Oklahoma City. Some Hornets fans feared their team would never return to New Orleans. The Hornets played just six games in New Orleans and 35 in Oklahoma City in 2006–07.

Oklahoma City did get an NBA team, but it wasn't the Hornets. The Seattle SuperSonics relocated there in 2008–09. New Orleans had gotten its team back a year earlier. The Hornets returned better than ever. With Paul established as one of the league's best players, they finished 56–26. The NBA held several activities in New Orleans to help rebuild the city. The All-Star Game was held at New Orleans Arena. Visiting teams and sponsors worked on several community service projects when they came to play the Hornets.

As the team improved, so did attendance. New Orleans even had a streak of 13 straight sellouts toward the end of the year. The fans were rewarded with the team's first playoff series victory. Paul led New Orleans to a 4–1 victory in the opening round over the Dallas Mavericks.

CHANGES IN NEW ORLEANS

Even with another playoff appearance a year later, the Hornets were in trouble. Shinn was losing money and could no longer afford to own the team. When he struggled to find a local buyer, fans worried the team might leave for good. Finally, the NBA bought the team.

Rewriting History

After the New Orleans Hornets changed their name to the Pelicans, the Charlotte Bobcats took the Hornets nickname back. Not only that, but Charlotte petitioned the league to give back the Pelicans' Charlotte history as well. Officially, the NBA now treats the Pelicans as a new team that started in 2002. They have no historical connection to Charlotte.

The bad news was that the Hornets could not afford to keep star players. Paul was traded after the 2010–11 season. Without their leader, the Hornets sank out of playoff contention.

When new owner Tom Benson took over in April 2012, he wanted to make more changes. He started with the team's name. The nickname "Hornets" had deep roots in Charlotte. It didn't mean much to New Orleans. Benson wanted something local. In January 2013 he announced that the new team name was "Pelicans" after the Louisiana state bird.

Right before the new name came a new star. The Hornets won the NBA Draft lottery in 2012. The prize was Anthony Davis. The imposing center became an All-Star in his second season. Davis's scoring ability made him a force at one end, while his rebounding and shot blocking kept opponents out of the lane.

Those skills also helped the Pelicans get back to the playoffs in 2014–15. Fans hoped it was the start of a team on the rise. But New Orleans lost in the first round. The Pelicans didn't make it back to the postseason for another three years.

In 2018 the pair of Davis and powerful center DeMarcus Cousins led New Orleans back to the postseason. They won a round but once again lost in the Western Conference semifinals. Davis was a perennial All-Star but became frustrated with his lack of help. Halfway through the next season he asked for a trade.

Davis finished the year in New Orleans, but his trade came through in July. The superstar was shipped to the Los Angeles Lakers for three players and three draft picks.

One of the players was young forward Brandon Ingram. And when the Pelicans won the draft lottery in 2019, they grabbed forward Zion Williamson. Suddenly the team was loaded with young, exciting players. New Orleans fans hoped it would be the group that could make the Pelicans into contenders.

Rookie Anthony Davis's 25 points, eight rebounds, six steals, and six blocks led New Orleans to its first victory as the Pelicans. They beat the Charlotte Bobcats 105–84 on November 2, 2013.

CHAPTER THREE

BOURBON STREET BALLERS

The Pelicans had two stars already on the roster when they moved from Charlotte to New Orleans in 2002. Forward Jamal Mashburn enjoyed the best year of his career in 2002–03. He averaged 21.6 points and 6.1 rebounds. That was good enough for his only career All-Star appearance.

Point guard Baron Davis had been the Hornets' first-round draft pick in 1999. When the team moved, he was just coming into his own. He made the All-Star team in 2003–04. That season Davis led the NBA in steals while also averaging a career-high 22.9 points per game.

The only thing that kept Mashburn and Davis from greater stardom was injuries. A knee injury kept Mashburn out of the lineup for most of 2003–04 and all of the next season. Davis struggled with several small injuries during his three

New Orleans forward Jamal Mashburn puts up a layup against the Los Angeles Lakers during a game in December 2002.

Pistol Pete

The Pelicans retired the No. 7 jersey of Pete Maravich during their first game in 2002. Maravich never played for this franchise. The man nicknamed "Pistol Pete" was a college star at Louisiana State University and played for the New Orleans Jazz for five years from 1974–75 to 1978–79. The Pelicans beat the Utah Jazz the day Maravich's jersey was retired.

years in New Orleans. He never played more than 67 games in any season.

The first era of New Orleans Hornets basketball came to a quick end on February 24, 2005. That day Davis was traded to the Golden State Warriors. Mashburn was traded to the Philadelphia 76ers. The forward never played in the NBA again due to chronic knee injuries.

PICK-AND-ROLL PAIR

The two players who led the best era in New Orleans Hornets history took very different paths to the NBA. Point guard Chris Paul was supposed to be a star. Power forward David West was not.

The Hornets took Paul fourth overall after finishing 18–64 in 2004–05. He had led Wake Forest to the top spot in the college basketball polls during his career. Joining the NBA didn't slow him down at all. Paul was named NBA Rookie of the Year. All but one of 125 voters wrote Paul's name on the ballot.

On the defensive end, Paul made life miserable for opposing point guards. Starting in 2007–08, he led the NBA

David West, *right*, and Chris Paul both averaged more than 20 points per game in 2007–08 as the Hornets finished 56–26.

in steals six of the next seven years. He also led the league in assists twice during his time in New Orleans.

Paul picked up many of those assists running the pick-and-roll with West. The power forward had been a mid-first-round pick in 2003 out of Xavier University in Cincinnati, Ohio. However, he didn't play much during his first two years in the NBA. Once Paul joined the roster, West's career took off. The two worked one of basketball's oldest plays to near perfection. West went from scoring 6.2 points per game in 2004–05 to more than 17 per game once he started setting screens for Paul.

The only problem for New Orleans fans was that Paul and West blossomed while the team was playing in Oklahoma City. When they finally returned to New Orleans for good in 2007–08, the pair was in high gear. Both players made the All-Star team. They also led New Orleans to its best record to date at 56–26.

The duo had help from rugged center Tyson Chandler and sweet-shooting Peja Stojaković. Things came together for the group in the playoffs. They knocked out the Dallas Mavericks in the first round before losing to the powerful San Antonio Spurs in seven games.

FEAR THE BROW

The University of Kentucky was enjoying a resurgence during the early 2010s. Never were they better than in 2012. Big man Anthony Davis led the way, earning college player of the year honors as a freshman. He went on to lead the Wildcats to the national title and was named Most Outstanding Player of the Final Four. The championship game that year was played in New Orleans. It turned out to be a preview for Hornets fans. The 6-foot-11-inch forward quickly became a force in the NBA.

Davis was a double-double machine. In seven years with the Hornets/Pelicans, Davis averaged a double-double six times. He was also one of the league's best shot-blockers.

With DeMarcus Cousins, *left*, and Anthony Davis, *right*, patrolling the lane, the Pelicans reached the playoffs for the first time in three years in 2017–18.

Davis also made headlines with his appearance. His bushy unibrow gained a lot of attention during his college days. Instead of trimming it, Davis profited from it. By the time his rookie year started, he had trademarked several phrases. One of them was "Fear the Brow."

While opponents feared his facial hair, Davis started to worry about a lack of help. Even his All-Star play couldn't get the Pelicans to the playoffs every year.

He finally got a running mate during the 2016–17 season. Center DeMarcus Cousins came over in a late-season trade. It wasn't enough to get the struggling Pelicans into the postseason that year. But Cousins and Davis formed a dominant duo the next season.

While Davis was long and skinny, Cousins was burly. He stood 6 feet, 10 inches and weighed 270 pounds. Cousins used his size to bull his way to the basket. As the Pelicans improved to 48–34 in 2017–18, Cousins averaged 25.2 points, 12.9 rebounds, and 5.4 assists.

Unfortunately, injury cut Cousins's season short. On January 26, 2018, Cousins had

Stat Stuffer

Four days before his fateful injury, DeMarcus Cousins put up 44 points, 23 rebounds, and 10 assists in a 132–128 victory over the Chicago Bulls. That made him the first player with 40 points, 20 rebounds, and 10 assists in the same game since legendary center Kareem Abdul-Jabbar in 1972.

a triple-double against the Houston Rockets. He did it in just 30 minutes before he tore his Achilles tendon. With Cousins lost for the season, the Pelicans had to play postseason basketball shorthanded.

The Pelicans still managed to reach the second round. A huge help was the play of guards Jrue Holiday and Rajon Rondo. Holiday had games of 33 and 41 points in the Pelicans' first-round sweep of the Portland Trail Blazers. Rondo averaged a double-double in the series, including 13.3 assists per game.

THE NEW FLOCK

Many fans thought the arrival of Zion Williamson might convince Anthony Davis to stay in New Orleans. That didn't happen. The forward was traded just days before Williamson was drafted. But New Orleans went from one star forward to another.

After missing the first half of his rookie season, Williamson took the league by storm in the second half. In 24 games he averaged 22.5 points per contest. Fans didn't get to see enough of him, though. The season was shut down in mid-March due to the COVID-19 pandemic. When play resumed in August, all games were played in one location, Orlando, Florida, to help the players isolate from the virus. The Pelicans were sent to the NBA bubble to play eight more games. If they had won enough of them, they could have made the playoffs. But they fell short

Brandon Ingram, *left*, drives against the Minnesota Timberwolves during a game in January 2022.

when Williamson missed three of the last four contests due to injury.

Williamson was back in 2020–21. His play was even better, at least when healthy. Williamson averaged 27.0 points per game and made his first All-Star team. However, like so many players in New Orleans team history, injuries hampered him again. He missed the final six games of the year with a fractured finger. The next fall, a broken bone in his foot caused him to miss the start of the 2021–22 season.

While Pelicans fans waited for Williamson to get healthy, Brandon Ingram blossomed into a star. At 6 feet, 8 inches and just 190 pounds, Ingram was nearly the opposite of Williamson. The small forward made his first All-Star team after coming to the Pelicans as part of the Davis trade. That year he was also named the Most Improved Player in the NBA.

Pelicans fans just wanted their two young stars on the court at the same time. Then the team could really take flight.

CHAPTER FOUR

BIG MOMENTS IN THE BIG EASY

Veteran forward Jamal Mashburn scored 50 points against the Memphis Grizzlies on February 21, 2003. The Hornets star needed all 50 of them to get the win.

The teams were tied 123–123 with the clock ticking down in overtime. Mashburn tried a running jumper but missed. The rebound fell to him, and his putback was the winning basket. On that night he hit 17 of 33 shots.

"I just knew that Mash would find a way (in the end)," Hornets coach Paul Silas said. "He had been finding a way all night. Mash took it upon himself to get it done. It was just magical. He did it all."

Mashburn's game was a New Orleans scoring record until Anthony Davis broke it. In 2016 Davis put up 59 points against the Detroit Pistons on 24-for-34 shooting. It came on February 21, exactly 13 years to the day after Mashburn's big game.

Jamal Mashburn made his only All-Star team in 2002–03, his first season in New Orleans.

Peja's Streak

Early in his first season with New Orleans, Peja Stojaković set an NBA record for consecutive points to start a game. Stojaković scored the Hornets' first 20 points against the Charlotte Bobcats on November 14, 2006. He finished with a career-high 42 points.

HOME SWEET HOME

Sports proved to be a huge part of getting New Orleans back to normal after the damage of Hurricane Katrina. Football's Saints returned in 2006 and treated fans to a playoff run. When the Hornets came back in 2007, they wanted to do the same.

The fans were ready as well. The Hornets played a few games in New Orleans while they were based in Oklahoma City. The first was on March 8, 2006, against the Los Angeles Lakers. A sellout crowd of 17,744 showed up to watch. It was the first major professional sporting event in the city since the hurricane.

"This is incredibly important," Louisiana governor Kathleen Blanco said. "It's not just a game. It's a real symbol of our ability to restore and renew ourselves and come back strong."

New Orleans lost that game, but the Hornets churned out wins in 2007–08. Back in New Orleans full time, Chris Paul and David West led the team to its first Southeast Division title.

In the opening round of the playoffs against the Dallas Mavericks, Paul put on a show. The Hornets trailed in Game 1,

Damage to New Orleans Arena, *far right*, from Hurricane Katrina kept the Hornets away from home for two seasons.

but Paul's 35 points and 10 assists led a 104–92 comeback win. He followed that up with 32 points and 17 assists in a Game 2 victory. No player had ever had at least 30 points and 10 assists in each of his first two career playoff games.

The Hornets led 3–1 when the series came back to New Orleans in Game 5. Paul closed out the Mavericks with a triple-double. In addition to his 24 points and 15 assists, he added 11 rebounds.

The Hornets then faced the defending champion San Antonio Spurs in the second round. Led by Paul's four double-doubles, the series went seven games. That's where the Hornets' magic ran out. Despite 16 points in the fourth

Chris Paul attacks the basket during Game 1 of the Hornets' 2008 playoff series victory over the Dallas Mavericks.

quarter from backup New Orleans guard Jannero Pargo, San Antonio held on for a 91–82 win.

DAVIS'S BIG SHOW

Davis made his first All-Star Game in 2014. That year the contest was held in New Orleans. Coming off the bench, the young forward scored 10 points.

Three years later the game came back to New Orleans. This time Davis was a starter. By the end of the night, he was the star among stars. The previous All-Star scoring record of 42 points was held by Hall of Famer Wilt Chamberlain. He set it in 1962.

For most of the night in 2017 it looked like Chamberlain's record was in trouble. With 7:54 left, Oklahoma City Thunder guard Russell Westbrook hit a three-pointer. The shot gave him 41 points. Less than two minutes later, Davis powered home a dunk for his forty-second point. Westbrook's assist set him up.

Pelicans center Anthony Davis holds up the MVP trophy from the 2017 All-Star Game.

Davis wasn't done. Late in the game he came down on a fast break with Golden State Warriors guard Steph Curry. Davis took Curry's lob off the backboard and slammed it. On the next possession Houston Rockets guard James Harden ran the same play. That dunk gave Davis a new record of 52 points.

"It was amazing. That's what I wanted to do," Davis said after the game. "Get the MVP for this crowd, for this city. This one means a lot to me."

The next season Davis set a more meaningful record for New Orleans. The team was back in the playoffs and facing the

Portland Trail Blazers. The Pelicans took a 3–0 lead in the series. Like Paul a decade earlier, Davis turned in a big game to close it out. His 47 points set a Pelicans playoff record. Davis scored 12 points in the final five minutes as New Orleans finished off the 131–123 victory. It was just the second playoff series win in team history.

NEARLY PERFECT

On February 12, 2021, the Pelicans traveled to Dallas for a matchup with the Mavericks. The game featured two of the NBA's best young stars, forwards Luka Dončić of Dallas and New Orleans' Zion Williamson.

The young guns did not disappoint. Both players finished the night with career-high point totals. Dončić scored 46 to lead Dallas to a 143–130 victory. But Williamson's 36-point effort was historic.

New Orleans' young star made a statement right away. Williamson dunked home the game's first two points just 1:07 into the first quarter. Later in the first he finished back-to-back possessions with two thunderous jams.

At the end of the first half, Williamson was 10-for-10 from the field. Every shot had been either a slashing layup or a dunk. The Mavericks could not keep the quick, powerful forward away from the basket.

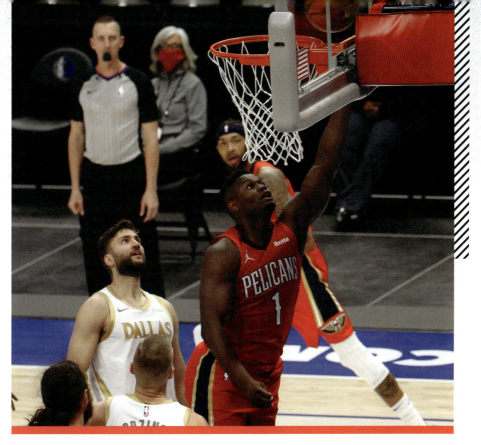

Zion Williamson lays in two of his 36 points against the Dallas Mavericks on February 12, 2021.

After the game, Dallas coach Rick Carlisle praised the young star. "Williamson was ridiculous," Carlisle said. "I mean, unbelievable, what he can do on a basketball floor."

What Williamson could not do on the night was miss shots. Every attempt went in until he tried a three-pointer roughly halfway through the third quarter. When the game ended, Williamson was 14-for-15 from the field. The 20-year-old was the youngest player ever to score 30 points on 90 percent shooting in an NBA game. It was something Pelicans' fans hoped to see for years to come.

TIMELINE

2002
The Hornets relocate to New Orleans after spending 14 seasons in Charlotte.

2004
The Hornets hire Byron Scott as head coach. He eventually leads the team back to the playoffs with a 56–26 record in 2007–08.

2005
The Hornets finish 18–64 and select point guard Chris Paul fourth overall in the NBA Draft.

In August, Hurricane Katrina devastates the New Orleans area, and the Hornets move to Oklahoma City for the next two seasons.

2007
The Hornets move back to New Orleans full-time to begin the 2007–08 season.

2008
The Hornets defeat the Dallas Mavericks to win their first playoff series since moving to New Orleans.

2010
The NBA buys the team from original owner George Shinn.

2011
The Hornets trade Paul to the Los Angeles Clippers.

2012
The Hornets are purchased by New Orleans Saints owner Tom Benson and draft Anthony Davis first overall.

2013
The team changes its name to the Pelicans.

2017
Davis scores a record 52 points in the All-Star Game played at Smoothie King Center.

2019
The Pelicans trade Davis to the Los Angeles Lakers and draft Zion Williamson first overall.

2020
Williamson makes his NBA debut and scores 17 points in less than four minutes of play in the fourth quarter.

TEAM FACTS

FRANCHISE HISTORY
New Orleans Hornets
 (2002–2005, 2007–13)
New Orleans/Oklahoma City
 Hornets (2005–2007)
New Orleans Pelicans (2013–)

KEY PLAYERS
Anthony Davis (2012–19)
Baron Davis (2002–05)
Jrue Holiday (2013–20)
Brandon Ingram (2019–)
Jamal Mashburn (2002–04)
Chris Paul (2005–11)
David West (2003–11)
Zion Williamson (2019–)

KEY COACHES
Alvin Gentry (2015–20)
Byron Scott (2004–10)

HOME ARENAS
Smoothie King Center (2002–)
 Formerly known as:
 New Orleans Arena (2002–12)
Ford Center (Oklahoma City)
 (2005–07)
Pete Maravich Assembly
 Center (Baton Rouge) (2005)

TEAM TRIVIA

WELCOME GUESTS

Although the team missed the playoffs both seasons, the Hornets averaged 18,300 fans at the Ford Center during 71 home games played in Oklahoma City.

CURTAIN CALL

After deciding to return to New Orleans for the 2007–08 season, the Hornets played one preseason game in Oklahoma City as a goodbye. New Orleans knocked off the Houston Rockets 94–92.

NAME GAME

Other names suggested for the Hornets' name change were Brass, a reference to the city's musical tradition, and Krewe. In New Orleans, a "krewe" is a social club. Many krewes are involved in planning parades for the city's famous Mardi Gras festival.

FIRST IN THE FRENCH QUARTER

Neither the Hornets nor the Jazz were the first professional basketball team in New Orleans. The New Orleans Buccaneers played in the American Basketball Association (ABA) from 1967 to 1970. The ABA was founded in 1967 to rival the NBA. The Buccaneers finished 48–30 their first season and lost the ABA Finals to the Pittsburgh Pipers. By 1971 the team had moved to Memphis, Tennessee.

GLOSSARY

assist
A pass that leads directly to a basket.

double-double
Accumulating 10 or more of two certain statistics in a game.

draft
A system that allows teams to acquire new players coming into a league.

franchise
A sports organization, including the top-level team and all minor league affiliates.

meniscus
A piece of cartilage that is located behind the kneecap.

overtime
An extra period of play when the score is tied after regulation.

rebound
When a player catches the ball after a shot has been missed.

rookie
A professional athlete in his or her first year of competition.

steal
When a player takes the ball from a player on the other team.

triple-double
Accumulating 10 or more of three certain statistics in a game.

MORE INFORMATION

BOOKS

Flynn, Brendan. *The NBA Encyclopedia for Kids*. Minneapolis, MN: Abdo Publishing, 2022.

Mahoney, Brian. *GOATs of Basketball*. Minneapolis, MN: Abdo Publishing, 2022.

Ybarra, Andres. *Great Basketball Debates*. Minneapolis, MN: Abdo Publishing, 2019.

ONLINE RESOURCES

To learn more about the New Orleans Pelicans, please visit **abdobooklinks.com** or scan this QR code. These links are routinely monitored and updated to provide the most current information available.

INDEX

Ball, Lonzo, 10–12
Benson, Tom, 22
Blanco, Kathleen, 36

Carlisle, Rick, 41
Chamberlain, Wilt, 38–39
Chandler, Tyson, 28
Cousins, DeMarcus, 23, 30–31
Curry, Steph, 39

Davis, Anthony, 22–23, 28, 30–31, 33, 35, 38–40
Davis, Baron, 17, 19, 25–26
DeRozan, DeMar, 10
Dončić, Luka, 40

Floyd, Tim, 17–18

Gentry, Alvin, 9, 11–12

Harden, James, 39
Holiday, Jrue, 31

Ingram, Brandon, 12, 23, 33

Jackson, Mark, 11
Johnson, Larry, 16

Mashburn, Jamal, 17–19, 25–26, 35
Melli, Nicolò, 9, 11
Mourning, Alonzo, 16

Pargo, Jannero, 38
Paul, Chris, 19–22, 26–28, 36–37, 40

Rondo, Rajon, 31

Scott, Byron, 18
Shinn, George, 15, 17, 19, 21
Silas, Paul, 17, 35
Stojaković, Peja, 28, 36

West, David, 26–28, 36
Westbrook, Russell, 39
Williamson, Zion, 5–6, 9–12, 23, 31–33, 40–41

ABOUT THE AUTHOR

Tom Glave learned to write about sports at the University of Missouri. He has written about sports for newspapers in New Jersey, Missouri, Arkansas, and Texas. He has also written several books about sports. He looks forward to teaching his four children about all sports.